Confessions of a Coffee Cup Collector

Adventures of Laughter, Faith and Coming Alive

Jennifer Hand

Table of Contents

Special Thanks

Friends, I have to start this with a SUPER BIG special thanks to my editor Casey Bagley. The back story is God laid on my heart to write this book and release it at a five year celebration party for Coming Alive Ministries. To have the book released by then, I needed to 1) write it in a week (Ps: my hands still hurt from all the typing 2) ask my incredible editor friend Casey Bagley to edit it in a week. Friends, she crafted my words in such beauty IN A WEEK and I am just so grateful.

And then there is the AMAZING (I keep having to use all caps because I get excited) Coming Alive Board of Directors. I could not imagine doing this ministry dream without you. So grateful for your behind the scenes help, your putting up with my crazy plans, and the way Jesus uses you in **all the things.** Thanks Casey and Barry Lewis, JP and Catrina Pruitt, Houston Gibson, Michelle and Todd Humbert, Brittany and Justin Smith, Don and Debbie Sapp—I love you guys.

And my awesome parents Mike and Vicky Hand who have been amazing cheerleaders and made growing up in their house the best thing ever!!

And to the incredible tribe of supporters who has supported Coming Alive Ministries for the past five years—I am so grateful for your prayers, your financial support and for you joining me on this journey of Coming Alive.

Chapter One

Coffee cup Confessions

Fifty-six plus a few more cracked ones that I cannot seem to bring myself to throw away. This is particularly unfortunate in the pre-coffee mornings when I forget about said cracks and pour steaming hot coffee into that broken mug—again.

Fifty-six is the number that I have whittled my coffee cup collection down to. The last time I moved, my friend told me that I had to get rid of every coffee cup that did not have a story. All the ones left have a story. Fat ones, skinny ones, from-all-around-the-world ones, pottery ones, dollar store ones, hope-I-don't-forget-I-can't-put-THAT-one-in-the-microwave ones. Each of these survived the Great Coffee Cup Purge of 2015. I am not even going to tell you how many I had before that because, well, it's the first few paragraphs of this book, and you don't know me that well. I don't want you to be distracted thinking that I need to go to Hoarders Anonymous simply because I only own a few bowls but have dozens of mugs. Don't worry. You can for sure eat ice cream out of my coffee mugs.

I feel like I should stop here and let you know that you do not have to collect coffee mugs to join me on this little journey. You do not even have to like coffee. *I promise I will not judge you if you do not like coffee. My own mom doesn't drink coffee. But I will pray for you a little extra because I feel you are missing out on one of God's greatest treasures—the coffee bean!* Perhaps you collect those fun little magnets and have the world's most awesomely decorated refrigerator. You may collect receipts and actually remember to enter them in somewhere. (I keep them, and I have no idea why. I don't enter them anywhere. Honestly, it just seems like the adult thing to do.) You may collect airbrushed t-shirts, free pens that you get when you go to the bank, or recipes from watching the Food Network that you probably will never cook.

You may not collect any **thing,** but we are all collectors. We collect memories—the scenes and stories that make up our lives. Memories of hilarious adventures filled with mishaps. (I, for one, have collected many of these.) Mental pictures of faces that changed us forever. And there are those memories we wish we could pack tightly in a box and drop off at the Goodwill.

Our lives are a series of stories. I am not sure when yours began. (In case you were wondering, mine began on March 15, 1982, one minute before my twin sister's did.) I don't know when it will end or what the stories will hold in the middle. But I do know the One who is writing these stories. The One who is giving you these collections of memories that make up your days.

God.

That moment felt sacred somehow. Just writing the name. God. Period.

Psalm 139 tells us about the moments that He is collecting in your life.

"Where shall I go from your Spirit? Or where shall I flee from your presence? If I ascend to heaven, you are there! If I make my bed in Sheol, you are there! If I take the wings of the morning and dwell in the uttermost parts of the sea, even

there your hand shall lead me, and your right hand shall hold me. If I say, 'Surely the darkness shall overcome me and the light about me be night,' even the darkness is not dark to you; the night is as bright as the day for darkness is as light with you.

For you formed my inward parts; you knitted me together in my mother's womb. I praise you for I am fearfully and wonderfully made. Wonderful are your works, my soul knows it very well.

My frame was not hidden from you, when I was being made in secret, intricately woven in the depths of the earth.

Your eyes saw my unformed substance; in your book were written, every one of them, the days that were formed for me, when as yet there were none of them."

Friends, I have read this passage hundreds of times. But tonight, as I was typing these words, I wanted to weep and shout, "Glory!" However, since I am in a coffee shop, I did neither. But I did fling my hands in the air a bit.

(Side note: I feel like you should know that I am trying to be one of those trendy authors right now. I hear all the rage is the standing desk. So, I am standing at the table at the coffee shop while typing. I have never tried it before... but frankly, I feel trendy and cool.)

Not only is your life a collection of stories and people and pictures and places and smells and experiences—but God, the author of YOUR story is weaving your story into HIS story.

Glory! (I couldn't help it there.)

Do you know that God sees you? That He knows you? That He loves you?

3

These seem like such simple phrases, but they are powerful, life-changing truths that I am trying to live in recognition of every day.

The God who sees and numbers the stars sees me and you. In fact, Matthew 10:30 tells us that even the hairs of our head are numbered.

He sees you. He sees the lies our hearts collect. He sees the truths we are fighting to believe instead. He sees us in those moments when we feel most unseen and unnoticed. He sees us in those moments we don't want anyone to notice. He sees us in the moments we want everyone to notice.

He knows you. 1 Corinthians 8:3 says , "But if anyone loves God He is known by God." I think inside all of us is the secret desire to be known. To be known is to feel understood. To feel important. To be noticed for who you are and not for who everyone else is.

Honestly, it could scare us all a bit that the God of the universe knows us and sees us. It brings to mind the song about Santa Claus that parents use to bribe their children to behave leading up to Christmas.

"He sees you when you're sleeping. He knows when you're awake. He knows if you've been bad or good so be good for goodness' sake."

It can be easy for us to fall into the trap of thinking that God is like a cosmic Santa Claus, watching for when we have been bad or good—and that how we land on the Naughty or Nice List changes how He sees us. This could make us very afraid that He knows us.

But………

4

This...is...the...kicker. The cream in the coffee. The thing that changes everything.

He loves you. Romans 8:35-39 says, "Who shall separate us from the love of Christ? Shall tribulation, or distress, or persecution, or famine, or nakedness, or danger, or sword? No, in all these things we are more than conquerors through Him who loved us. For I am sure that nothing, neither death nor life, nor angels nor rulers, nor things present nor things to come, nor powers, nor height nor depth, nor anything else in all creation, will be able to separate us from the love of God in Christ Jesus."

The Costa Rican Coffee Cup

Can I talk with you for a moment about my Costa Rican coffee cup? It's the most recent addition to my collection so it makes sense we talk about it first. It's made from a sort of clay (I think—totally guessing) with a butterfly, a parrot, and a weird looking sloth on it. I picked it because of the way it felt in my hands.

That's a big thing when picking out a coffee mug.

A few weeks ago, God opened the door for me to go on a trip to Costa Rica. The trip was chock full of memories my heart collected that I pray changed me forever.

Like how He humbled me and reminded me of the beautiful body of Christ. I generally travel overseas alone, and this was with a group from my church. A group of very different personality types. I am a fly by the seat of my pants, just make sure there is time for coffee kind of girl. So, to be honest, I was dreading the idea of a schedule, of not flying by the seat of my pants, of wondering how our eclectic group of personalities would mesh.

But I watched God make us a family. First Corinthians 12 describes the body of Christ as a beautiful body with parts that all work together. This is how the bride of Christ was created to be.

On our trip, we had Teresa who was very organized and took care of all the details. We had Jake who had studied up on Spanish and did an amazing job communicating. His awesome wife Maggie was on the team also. Together they led an incredible kids program that I could have never thought up. My pastor, Chris, shepherded our entire team beautifully and poured into the Costa Rican pastors in powerful ways. Kevin and Sarah were on their first mission trip where I have lost count of the number of trips I have been on overseas— but they taught me so much about faith and stepping out of your comfort zone.

Evan came to do video for our trip—but his equipment was all stolen in our first few hours there. He showed us the power of faith and counting it all joy when he kept trusting that God was somehow in that story.

Jordan made me laugh – all the time—and I could tell he was created for the adventure of mission work.

Glenna is a powerhouse of the Spirit, and our conversations at night changed me.

Then there was Paul who owns a wildlife removal company. Talking to him was fascinating, especially when he shared about the hundreds of times he had been bitten by snakes. (*I know right!)* He was the best listener and question-asker. I will never forget the question he asked around the lunch table about the thin places we have experienced in our lives. The Holy Spirit showed up as the team shared, and it was a moment of sacred holiness.

And the Vaughan family—the missionaries we came to work with. Two years ago, they took a risk. They told us how they were not risk takers before. They liked sameness. Comfort. Knowing.

But God saw them, He knew them ,and, in His love for them, He called them.

And He saw those in Costa Rica and knew them and loved them. So He called the Vaughan family to go for them.

This family loves deep in a way I have not seen before. They walk in the power of the Holy Spirit—but in such a gentle, humble, exciting way that it made all of us want MORE of God and His glory that was shining so brightly through their story.

That week in Costa Rica humbled me. (*Speaking of humbling, can I tell you that I don't speak Spanish, but I was trying to tell my new friend I loved her coffee. Apparently I was emphatically telling her that my name was "coffee" in Spanish.*) I so often want to collect moments in my story that are not for His glory, but for Jenn's story. "Look at what Jenn is doing for Jesus." "Look at how God is using her." I can quickly gain a sense of worth in what I think is my WORK. That week, I watched God work through my friends and was reminded again God doesn't *need* me. He *wants* me. He delights in His children working together to display Him.

I watched God see us, know us, and love us.

I think that is why I wanted to share those phrases with you.

Seen.

Known.

Loved.

 I cannot get them out of my head. Each morning, when I have my coffee (in the new sloth mug), I ask God to help me to live out my day wrapped tightly in those truths so that I don't live bound in insecurity and lies.

While in Costa Rica, we had the joy of going to some very remote houses where I am sure it would be easy for the people to feel unseen. Adam and Kelly, the missionaries there, have built a framework where they remind the people they encounter that they are loved by God. We were blessed to join that framework and take that love to families in need.

My favorite thing was going to the homes of the local people. We brought groceries to meet physical needs, but, as we gathered around, we would ask how we could pray for them. We reminded them that God sees them, knows them, and loves them.

Many had physical struggles that we could visibly see. I loved when our hands mingled together, each touching the person we were praying for so they were reminded that God wants to touch them.

And we prayed. Together. In the name of Jesus.

And I want to tell you—We saw Him come. Visible healings came. Physical and emotional healings...they came.

And with each mustard seed of faith, we saw God move a mountain.

If we were having coffee together right now, I would ask you in what ways you have experienced being seen by God, loved by God, known by God.

How about this? Will you find someone to answer that question with? Will you sit with it? Will you pray through it? Will you ask God to show you the ways that maybe you have forgotten that you are seen, loved, and known? (*Because, let's be honest here, we can easily find ourselves forgetting.*)

"But now thus says the Lord, he who created you, O Jacob, he who formed you O Israel; 'Fear not, for I have redeemed you; I have called you by name, you are mine.'" (Isaiah 43:1)

I cannot wait for us to take the rest of this adventure together. As we think about adventures of faith, the mundane moments, and the in-between, let's celebrate that the God who authored our moments is collecting them with us. (*I wonder if God scrapbooks in heaven. I would love it if, when we reach heaven, He hands us each our scrapbook complete with themed stickers and the perfect scrapbook paper. In my mind, I want to be crafty and have things like scrapbooks here. But the reality is that I only have one partially completed scrapbook where the glue is rotting off the pictures, and it looks like it was made by a child rather than an eighteen year old.*)

Chapter Two

The God-sized Dream Coffee Mugs

I always like to imagine that you are right here with me while I write. One of my favorite things that people say to me is that, while they were reading my book, they felt like they could hear my voice in the words (and I am hoping my laugh, too). Truthfully, I want this to feel like a coffee shop conversation where we share our hearts, lattes (if you are the coffee drinking type), and deep belly laughs.

If you were here right now, you would be seated next to me in a swanky coffee shop in Midtown Atlanta. I mean, how fancy does that sound? Any town that has a Midtown is fancy for me. I tried to walk in here like I was trendy and a hipster, but I actually didn't even know where you even ordered the coffee. And if it hadn't been for my GPS, I would have had no idea how to get here in the first place. (I always pray that the sweet little lady in my phone who tells me turn by turn where to go doesn't quit. She has to recalculate a lot because I do a very bad job of following her directions.)

But here I am now, with my I-am-not-quite-sure-what-I-ordered steaming coffee—and you.

I imagine you have found yourself at one time or another wanting to be somewhere and are not quite sure how to get there. Or perhaps you find yourself looking for a pit stop in between where you are and where you want to be.

What do you dream about? What do you feel like you were placed on earth to do?

Do you still dream? Or do you find yourself deciding that dreaming is too hard?

Are you at a crossroads wondering which way to turn: right or left? Or maybe you know the right way is forward but going backward seems much more safe and smart?

Have you taken steps toward seeing a God-sized dream fulfilled only to become completely overwhelmed and decide that normal life is much easier than dreaming life?

I realize that was a series of a lot of questions. Let's just take a moment and pause here. Really. Sometimes it's easy to want to skip over hard questions or pretend we know the answers when we don't. Or is that just me here, friends?

(Since we are pausing, I am going to take a long, dramatic sip of my fancy-schmancy coffee that I wasn't even sure what I ordered in this swanky coffee place.)

Dreams, Directions, and Detours

One of the most often quoted verses I hear is Jeremiah 29:11. I love it also. It is a powerful promise filled with encouraging truths to cling to.

"For I know the plans I have for you, declares the Lord, plans for wholeness and not for evil to give you a future and a hope."

I wonder if you happen to know the context of this verse? I will be honest, I had to dig a little deeper and brush up on the context when I knew I was going to ask you that question. Because I think it's important for us to know this is not just a coffee cup worthy verse. (Can you see it now with

12

the new and stylish hand lettering? *Jeremiah 29:11.* Then underneath it the word *#hope* in those trendy updated fonts?)

This passage is found in a letter written by the prophet Jeremiah. Jeremiah 29 verse 1 tells us, "These are the words of the letter that Jeremiah the prophet sent from Jerusalem to the surviving elders of the exiles and to the priests, the prophets, and all the people whom Nebuchadnezzar had taken into exile from Jerusalem to Babylon."

So, these words of hope and future were written in a letter to people **in exile.** They had not only been defeated by the enemy, they had been captured and carried away.

Have you ever felt that? Defeated? Like someone came and captured your dreams and carried them away? Sometimes, we can even feel like our destiny has been captured. Like THAT mistake keeps us from experiencing our dream.

Or we become afraid that we dreamed the wrong dream, took the wrong detour, got lost and the GPS quit working on us.

Or we don't trust the directions we are being given and go on a different route. (Anyone else ever doubt the GPS lady ?)

Jeremiah 29:11 was written as a verse of hope for those who, I imagine, were feeling slightly hopeless. The dream of the Promised Land was feeling like a far off promise. The Lord was telling them, "I will fulfill my promise and bring you back—in my time and my way." The Lord even tells them how long. He says 70 years. I think it's a good thing the Lord doesn't tend to give us numbers like that nowadays. I think it could be a bit hard for this gal who doesn't always enjoy waiting to think I was going to have to wait for my dream for 70 years. It's best for me just not to know.

Truthfully, we are not to spend our lives simply waiting on a dream. We are to spend our lives watching the Dream Maker. (God is the Dream Maker in case you need a little hint. I mean, sometimes I convince myself it is me. But well—praise JESUS it's not. The One who I get to watch, and wait on, and worship is Jesus!)

Our dream giver is the Dream Maker.

You may have taken a detour. You may find yourself lost. You may find yourself right in the middle of a God-sized dream that feels too big, too overwhelming, too much.

Or you may feel pretty comfortable. You may consider yourself to not be that much of a dreamer and wonder how you can you relate to this chapter.

Wherever you find yourself, this is the amazing thing I was reminded of as I read Jeremiah 29:11. Continue on to verse 12.

"Then you will call upon me and come and pray to me and I will hear you. You will seek me and find me when you seek me with all your heart. I will be found by you, declares the Lord, and I will restore your fortunes and gather you from all the nations and all the places where I have driven you, declares the Lord, and I will bring you back."

This was a promise that God was giving to the Israelite people who were in exile, but it is an amazing promise for us today. This is an "I got so excited I almost spilled my coffee (again)" kind of promise.

When we seek Him, we will find Him.

When we pray, He hears. He responds.

He sees you. He knows you. He loves you.

He sees your dreams.

He sees your fears about your dreams.

He sees those of you that cringe at the word *dream*.

He sees those of you that feel your dreams are too small and don't matter at all. (There is Dr. Seuss rhyme for you.)

He sees you when you feel your dreams are way too big and your inadequacies are bigger still.

Babylon may have felt like a detour to those Jeremiah was called to be a prophet to, but God already had the re-route planned.

When we seek Him, we find direction from Him. His voice may not be audible like the GPS lady, but His word still speaks. It's alive and active.

"Your word is a light to my feet and a light to my path."
(Psalm 119:105)

One of my favorite coffee mugs is the prettiest color of teal blue. (At least I think that is what color you would call it. I hope you don't get your color wheel out on me.) It has a quote by one of my favorite authors on it.

"Dare to make that difference, take that step, follow that dream."
~ Holley Gerth

When I take a sip of steaming hot coffee from that mug, I look at the picture on it. It has a birdcage on it that is open with a bird taking flight.

I do not want my dreams, which I pray are God's dreams, to stay caged because I am afraid, scared to start, unsure, or detoured.

I want to fly.

And I imagine you want to fly.

What is your first step? I don't know. I wish I could tell you. I admit that I wish you could tell *me* what *my* next step is. I think mine is trusting the goodness of God. Trusting Psalm 16:11, "that He will make known to me the path of life, that in His presence is fullness of joy, at His right hand are pleasures forevermore."

And out of that trust, taking the next ministry steps He has called me to, even though they both overwhelm me and excite me. (And make me sweat just a little more.)

Your first step might be not stepping at all. It might be stopping. Kneeling. Asking. Seeking.

It might be making that scary phone call. It might be opening the closed door of your heart to dream again.

It might be typing those words on your keyboard for that e-mail or that book.

It might be trusting God with your children and the dreams He has for them.

I have such a sense of urgency for you as I type these words. Almost a heaviness in my Spirit. I so want you to trust God's dreams for your life. Just as I want to deeply trust God's dreams for my life.

I want us to know that our good Father has good things in store. That we can trust Him for direction. That we can trust Him for dreams. That we can trust Him for God-ordained detours.

Cups of Dreamers

I have several coffee mugs that represent my friends who have dared to dream.

I have one that has a beautiful logo and the word "with" on it. You see, I have a dear friend who, a few years ago, stepped aside from the ministry she had always known and loved for a dream of forming a ministry God was birthing in her heart.

She wanted to introduce people to the concept of "with," inviting people to show up and be present in each other's lives, to listen and be attentive to God. There was one day she came to my house to dream about what it would look like to start her own non-profit organization. I had the joy of being WITH her when she filled out the first of the paperwork to do just that, pushing send on the computer, stepping out even with fears and unanswered questions.

Then there is the mug that says, "Brave as a Girl can Be." When I hug this mug (guys, I am a coffee cup snuggler), I pray for God to make me brave like my friend Deb Brown. She wrote an amazing book called, Brave as a Girl Can Be: Let's get off the Fear Cycle and Live Free. This book is a beautiful invitation to bravery. To letting go of our fears. It was a dream she watched God accomplish through her, even when she was afraid. (P.S. This is available on Amazon, and you need it!!)

I have several beautiful pottery mugs from different years of Winsome Retreats. This was a retreat founded by my dear friend Kim Hyland. God planted a seed of faith in her for a retreat that brought women of all ages and backgrounds together for a weekend of authenticity, diversity, and truth. I have been so blessed to see how God has used this dream to change women's lives forever.

And then there is this cup that has a Coming Alive Ministries logo on it. I remember when God first plopped the dream of Coming Alive Ministries in this girl's heart. I had no idea what it would look like, but I knew God was placing in me a dream to invite people to come alive and live alive in Christ.

I am praying for your dreams friend. I am praying Ephesians 3:20-21 over you.

"Now to him who is able to do far more abundantly than all that we ask or think, according to the power at work within us, to him be glory in the church and in Christ Jesus throughout all generations, forever and ever AMEN."

How is that for a dream?

Chapter Three

That Mug from the Dollar Tree

I feel like you should know something about me—I am a little bit of a cheap gal. I love me a good bargain. I learned that from my mom. She could buy one get one free *plus* use five coupons that she had so painstakingly cut out. Aldi is one of my favorite places to grocery shop. For those of you that don't know the glories of Aldi, it's a much cheaper place to buy groceries. Sure, you have to have a quarter to rent your buggy (or shopping cart for the non-southerners among us), and you have to bring your own bag, but it's a bargain.

I actually love what I call the Aldi pay-it-forward phenomenon. Often times, there will be someone exiting at the same time I am entering, and they give me their shopping cart with their quarter still in. There is still "leave your quarter in for the next guy" goodness in the world. It makes me smile, and I am certain it makes God smile. I mean, could there be a better way to love thy neighbor as thyself?

I especially love it for those times when I cannot find a quarter anywhere, and I try to convince myself I don't need a buggy anyways. That is until I am carrying all the things— which translates into *dropping* all the things. Including the eggs all over aisle five.

That may or may not have happened to me.

We will get to my favorite Dollar Tree mug I promise, but can I tell you that the other day I bought toilet paper from Aldi? I feel like I need to apologize to you in case you happen to come visit my house in the next few weeks.

I am a firm believer that you really shouldn't skimp and buy cheap toilet paper. Maybe because I grew up in a house where my mom always found coupons, so we always had the nice deluxe toilet paper.

But, to be honest, I am on the missionary budget, so Aldi's toilet paper it was this week.

I was in a hurry and noticed a big pack of 24 rolls of toilet paper that was a steal of a deal, so I bought it.

In my car, on the way home I kept thinking, "Something in my car smells really weird. Like a mixture of bad Pine-sol and mothballs." I got home, unloaded my groceries, and grabbed the toilet paper.

Imagine my surprise when I realized it was the toilet paper that smelled of a bad mixture of cleaning products and mothballs. I had cheap, off-brand *lavender scented* toilet paper. Guys, I wish this book was scratch and sniff. Toilet paper should NOT be scented.

A good bargain shopper appreciates another good bargain shopper. A few Christmas's ago, my neighbor Sarah, who had become a dear friend, and I exchanged Christmas gifts. I had found the perfect cute coffee mug for her from the Dollar Tree. It had an adorable green tree on it. I bought it because it reminded me of what I had seen in Sarah— beautiful growth. The tree looked alive and vibrant and represented the faith I had seen Sarah develop.

I wrapped it in a Dollar Tree Christmas bag (Guys, if you happen to somehow not know, everything at the Dollar Tree is a dollar. It's amazing. You can get everything from a pack of off-brand Oreos to decorations for a party, to a toilet bowl cleaner – for a DOLLAR), and at the Christmas Eve brunch I was hosting, handed it to her.

She then handed me a gift, so we decided to open them at the same time.

Imagine our surprise and laughter when we both reached into our bags and pulled out **the exact same coffee mugs**.

Don't you love that moment when you do not have to worry about even taking off the price tag (well, there aren't price tags at the Dollar Tree because everything is a dollar) because you bought each other the same gift!

Can I tell you what is so cool about my friend Sarah? Well, there are so many things. You know how I mentioned that I bought the mug because it had a tree on it and I had seen so much growth in her? I lived in a quadruplex, which is a fancy way of saying a house that had been broken into four apartments. Sarah and Kevin lived on the other side of our apartment.

When I met Sarah, she did not have a relationship with Jesus. But before I tell you more about that, can I tell you about Zelda? On the top floor of the apartment that my roommate and I shared lived Zelda. You can read about Zelda in some of my other books. I feel like she deserves a mention in any book I write.

Zelda is an elderly spitfire of a woman. She often took her teeth out, especially when reading her Bible. At least that is what she told me one day. She informed me it was much easier to hear from Jesus when her teeth were not in. You never knew when Zelda would just pop in, or if her teeth would be in or out.

My first encounter with her was when I came out of the shower the first week I lived in my new apartment. I came out of my bathroom wrapped in a towel, and imagine my surprise when Zelda was standing there. She informed me that she had knocked on the door and I didn't answer so she came on in. She then informed me that I was parked in her parking spot, even though there are no designated parking spots.

Zelda loved to come down and knock on the door, her hands filled with some of the ingredients in a recipe but not all the ingredients you would need. For example, one night she brought me some spaghetti noodles and asked if I would go to the store, buy some meat, and make some homemade spaghetti.

My favorite memory was when she ran down in her nightgown and asked if I would make her a scrambled egg (scrambled easy, she made sure to point out) sandwich, lightly toasted, of course. Who knew I had signed up to be the innkeeper at a bed and breakfast? (By the way, she did not like the way my toaster lightly toasted.)

My roommate Emily and I, along with Sarah and Kevin on the other side, never quite knew what to expect from Zelda.

The Greatest Commandment

Jesus was asked by the Pharisees in Matthew 22:36-40 what the greatest commandment was.

"And he said to him, 'You shall love the Lord your God with all your heart and with all your soul and with all your mind. This is the great and first commandment. And a second is like it: You shall love your neighbor as yourself.'"

Sometimes, loving my neighbor meant making Zelda a lightly toasted scrambled egg sandwich or taking her to Walmart even without her teeth in.

Jesus' last words were a convicting commission. Not only has He already told us the second greatest commandment is to love our neighbor, He told us the word, "Go."

"And Jesus came and said to them, 'All authority in heaven and on earth has been given to me. Go therefore and make disciples of all nations, baptizing them in the name of the Father, and of the Son and of the Holy Spirit, teaching them to observe all that I have commanded you. And behold, I am with you always to the end of the age.'" (Matthew 28:18-20)

Wow, those are power packed last words.

Frankly, the adventurer in me loves the word **go**. That is part of the reason I have so many coffee mugs. I get one from every country I visit. I love that Jesus told us to go. I am always all about the go. Jesus where do you want to take me now? Here I am, send me.

I realize that we are all different. That there are some of you reading this that are like, "Um, one of the scariest things about becoming a Christian to me is that God may call me to a third world country to live in a hut and eat rice all the time."

I understand that too. Maybe you feel about that like I feel about the Lord calling me to a nine to five desk job. I want to be willing, but I pray that never happens.

There is something interesting in the account that Acts gives of Jesus' last words. It's a little bit more specific about this whole going thing.

"But you will receive power when the Holy Spirit has come upon you, and you will be my witnesses in Jerusalem and in all Judea and Samaria and to the ends of the earth."
(Acts 1:8)

Jesus told them to start just where they were. The going was not first to the ends of the earth. It was to Jerusalem— where they already were. To love their neighbors.

Love God, love your next door people. Your cashier at the grocery store people. Your coffee shop barista people. Your family people. And, as you love your people, share Jesus with your people.

Here is what I realized with my neighbor, Sarah. I loved her. Loved anytime I got to hang out with her, especially when we were in the driveway talking about our latest Zelda adventure. I wanted to move past just loving her and into sharing Jesus with her and Kevin, but I was afraid.

But listen, I had a roommate, Emily, who was brave and bold. She just did it. She built a relationship with them and went beyond just that relationship. She invited them to church. (Emily and I attended the same church. The one I had not been brave enough to invite them to.)

And they trusted her enough to come. And they met Jesus there. And guess what. You may remember them in Chapter One of this book. I got to GO on their first overseas mission trip with them.

I have seen God use them again and again. I have seen them grow (hence the green tree coffee mug story I gave you in the beginning which led to this entire chapter). Kevin became the outreach director, and I loved that, on the next Thanksgiving, not only did we both laugh because at different times we each took Zelda to Walmart, but I got to deliver Thanksgiving meals to those people Kevin had coordinated for us to minister to. I have watched them minister faithfully in the children's department at church. I loved watching them step out in faith and minister in Costa Rica.

I miss them desperately now that we are not neighbors anymore, especially on the nights when I leave my car interior light on. I used to often get texts from Kevin gently reminding me my car light was on. Again.

Kevin and Sarah recently signed up to be foster parents. How awesome is God? How awesome is God's story in their story? How could this have not become their story if Emily had not been brave in her own story?

How can you be brave in your story? Maybe it's taking your neighbor a Dollar Tree mug and reminding them (or telling them for the first time) that Jesus loves them.

Maybe it's saying, "God, I don't necessarily want to go, and it makes me shake in my boots (whatever that really means) to say this, but here I am. Send me."

Wherever, however, whatever—let's do a little loving God and, therefore, loving people.

Maybe God will even have you give that quarter to someone to rent their buggy at Aldi.

Chapter Four

Communion Cups

I grew up in a church that served communion in the silver trays with the tiny cups filled with grape juice and the thin wafers. Communion was always served by the deacons in their suits, and I was always terrified to do the balance and pass of the wiggly grape juice filled cups. I may or may not have spilled one all over the man next to me once.

Can I also tell you a weird confession about me? I used to love the taste of the grape juice.

(OK, let me tell you that, if you are a germophobe, do NOT read the next sentence. You may find yourself scarred for life.)

After church was over and before they collected the little cups, I went down the aisles licking them all. (And before you judge my parents, they had no idea I was doing it. I was sneaky and fast. All it took was one quick conversation to distract my mom, and I had done the deed.)

Some churches do what I call the rip and dip method. The "tear off a piece of bread and dip it in the cup" version of the "pass the silver tray" version that I grew up with.

Regardless of how you do it, there is something so sacred and holy and life-giving about communion.

It represents Christ's body—broken for you.

It represents Christ's blood—shed for you.

I have been to the site in Jerusalem they believe to be the Upper Room. I have stood in that place in the middle of the bustling streets of Jerusalem. What a sacred moment it was for me as I imagined Jesus gathered there with His disciples.

The sacredness of the moment ended a bit more quickly than I imagined when the nuns , who are now the keepers of the Upper Room, asked us to leave because we got a *little* excited in there and were singing a worship song. They apparently wanted the Upper Room to be the "quiet room."

In those moments, standing there, I imagined Jesus passing that cup. I pictured the confusion the disciples must have felt.

Jesus knew His blood must flow so His grace could flow.

He knew His body would be broken so that we could be made whole.

He knew what the disciples could not understand that this was all part of His glorious plan.

Would you go with me for a second to the Upper Room?

"Now as they were eating, Jesus took bread, and after blessing it broke it and gave it to the disciples and said, 'Take, eat, this is my body.' And he took a cup, and when He had given thanks he gave it to them, saying, 'Drink of it, all of you, for this is my blood of the covenant, which is poured out for many for the forgiveness of sins. I tell you I will not drink again of this fruit of the vine until that day when I drink it new with you in my Father's kingdom.'" (Matthew 26:26-30)

The Upper Room is a small, seemingly insignificant room tucked away in Jerusalem. But in this room, the disciples were offered a gift that would change everything.

The remembrance of what Christ was going to do for them.

As I stood in that room, I pictured again the cup being offered—this time to me.

Do this in remembrance of me, Jenn.

There is absolutely no cup of coffee in the world that I could drink that would change my life like this one.

I cannot imagine the day in heaven when Jesus himself passes the cup to me at the marriage supper of the lamb. (Just take a moment and read Revelation 19 friends. I know we can tend to shy away from Revelation because there is a great deal of confusing imagery and prophecy—but wow. The idea that the cup Jesus offered the disciples that day in the Upper Room is the same cup that contains my invitation to the marriage supper of the lamb—the Blood of Jesus. Well, glory!)

I have a beautiful communion cup that means more to me than any coffee mug ever will. It was a gift from a dear couple that I met while on my first trip to Israel. It is delicately carved out of olive wood—depicting Jesus and His disciples at the table eating the Last Supper.

This sweet couple had seen me admire it. I had only known them for that week, but they surprised me by purchasing it for my birthday, which I was blessed to get to celebrate in Israel.

I will never forget that birthday celebration. There are people from all over the world in the hotels in Jerusalem. The dining rooms are crazy-full of people and you join your group at the table with your group's designated name. There are massive buffet tables filled with all kinds of yummy and delicious Mediterranean food. Often, I had no idea what I was putting on my plate. A little of this stuffed olive, a sprinkle of feta cheese, some chicken (or is that lamb), and a French fry thrown in for good measure.

This couple had bought a surprise cake and had the wait staff come out with the cake singing, "Happy Birthday" with their thick Israeli accents. The Japanese folks at the table next to us very enthusiastically sang along at the top of their lungs.

I felt very celebrated.

The couple who was leading the team, dear friends of mine, had seen me admire an olive wood carved nativity set in Bethlehem. **I mean who would not want a nativity set that was actually carved in Bethlehem where the original nativity scene was?** This was their beautiful gift to me. What a treasure that I look at daily, reminding me that the Messiah, who came just as He promised, is a daily promise keeper.

Next, I opened the gift from the sweet couple that I had just met that week. The communion set took my breath away. I don't want to sound all cheesy and sentimental here, but well—I am going to anyway.

See, back in the day of Jesus, offering a woman the cup for communion was a way the groom asked to be her betrothed. Maybe that's why the disciples were more than perplexed when Jesus passed the cup to them.

That day at my birthday celebration, I felt Jesus propose to me all over again.

Friend, Jesus took the cup of suffering so we could take the cup and drink the living water. So that your sins and my sins could be washed clean by the power of His blood. Every day that we wake up, we get to drink from His new mercies.

"The steadfast love of the Lord never ceases; his mercies never come to an end; they are NEW every morning; great is your faithfulness. 'The Lord is my portion,' says my soul, 'therefore I will hope in Him.'" (Lamentations 3:22-24)

In the Garden

Jesus may have passed the cup to the disciples in the Upper Room at the Last Supper. But there was a day when Jesus did not pass the cup; He drank from it.

Let's move from the Upper Room to a simple little garden, also a seemingly insignificant place in the middle of bustling Jerusalem.

Jesus went with His disciples to this garden after leaving the Upper Room. The first time I visited this garden in Israel, I was not sure what to expect. It was simply a small garden with very old olive trees. These trees are the very trees that Jesus would have sat under.

The One who spoke those trees into being was going to stand under those trees and accept the cup of suffering.

We walked into the private part of the garden, where your group gets an appointment time to spend alone there.

I walked in on the last day of my 33rd year simply overwhelmed that this was the place where Jesus had spent the last day of His 33rd year also. (Truthfully, I was hoping that my day the next day did not end up quite the same way Jesus' did.) Our guide shared for a minute, we sang a hymn, and then we were released to go off by ourselves and spend time with Jesus.

It was truly the holiest of holy ground. I was undone. I blubber-sobbed. Not the cute attractive "she has small tears" kind of cries. The "get down on your knees, the dirt stuck to the sweat on your legs, overwhelmed by the love of God" kind of sobs.

On the last day of His 33rd year, Jesus was here. Choosing not to pass a cup, but to drink from it.

*"Then Jesus went with them to a place called Gethsemane, and he said to his disciples, 'Sit here, while I go over there and pray.' And taking with him Peter and the two sons of Zebedee, he began to be sorrowful and troubled. Then he said to them, 'My soul is very sorrowful, even to the death; remain here, and watch with me.' And going a little farther he fell on his face and prayed, saying, 'My Father, if it is possible, **let this cup pass from me;** nevertheless, not as I will, but as you will.' And he came to the disciples and found them sleeping. And He said to Peter, 'So, could you not watch with me one hour? Watch and pray that you may not enter into temptation. The Spirit indeed is willing, but the flesh is weak.' Again, for the second time, he went away and prayed, 'My Father, if this cannot pass unless I drink it, **your will be done.'"** (Matthew 26:36-42)*

In that garden, Jesus made a choice. To drink the cup of suffering. To bear our sins. To drip His blood that He might purify and cleanse us of those sins. He chose you. He chose me. He chose the cup.

I left that garden changed forever. I was chosen.

I pray that you are leaving the garden today knowing you were chosen by a Savior who took on the cross.

Later that day, we walked down the Via Delarosa, the way of the cross. I almost felt like I should take my shoes off. There is still a portion underground that is the original Roman road that Jesus would have taken heavy footsteps on, dragging the cross of shame behind Him.

Now the Via Delarosa takes you through a bustling marketplace with people everywhere selling this and that. In fact, you have to pay pretty close attention not to lose your group or your guide. Not that *I* would EVER lose my group or my guide.

As we were walking through the marketplace, I remember there was a man in our group randomly talking to me about how they grow cashews and why that makes them so expensive. Apparently, he had noticed some cashews in the market. I think he probably wondered why I had huge tears falling down my face. I mean, who doesn't get emotional about the cost of cashews in today's economy?

Big tears were falling because, as he was speaking about cashews, I realized that this was the center of town in Jesus' day. He would have had to walk through people. Lots of people.

I pictured Him as we walked. I pictured Him bloody from the beatings He had already received. I pictured the stares He was getting. The assumptions people were having. Here was a common criminal on the way to be crucified.

What they did not know was that the One carrying the cross for their sins was the only One who could really carry them because He had created them.

(OK, literally as I typed that, I had to pause and grab some tissues because it hit me all over again...my Creator carrying the cross of a criminal on the way to be crucified. The One who made the wood had been whipped and beaten by it.)

He chose to drag the cross of shame so that I never have to drag my own shame. He took on shame for me. For you. For the world.

We walked those streets to the place where they believe Jesus was crucified. Where He took His last breath. Where He laid in a tomb for three days. Where His body no longer is because He did what He promised. I love this In Matthew 28: 5-7:

*"But the angel said to the women, 'Do not be afraid, for I know that you seek Jesus who was crucified. He is not here, for he has risen **as he said.** Come, see the place where he lay. Then go quickly and tell his disciples that he has risen from the dead.'"*

I felt the same sort of anticipation Mary might have felt as she approached the tomb. There really are not adequate enough words to describe how it felt to walk in and sense the invitation. "Jenn, come and see the place where He lay; He is not here, for he has risen **as he said**."

I am so grateful Jesus is an "as He said" follow through kind of guy.

After I exited that empty tomb, I was handed a cup. It was not a coffee cup, but a tiny wooden communion cup. We went and had communion right there by the empty tomb.

Because He drank the cup of suffering, I can drink the cup of forgiveness.

He has risen as He said.

P.S. I do have a coffee cup from Israel that I bought at the gift shop in Jerusalem , of course!

Chapter Five

That One Time in an Airport

Friends, because I am blessed to travel a great deal with Coming Alive Ministries, I spend a lot of time in airports. Can we talk about airport people watching? It's fabulous. I mean, absolutely the best.

And, let's be honest, I have been the one that people have watched at times and probably never forgotten.

Many of my mugs from other states or countries that I have traveled to have been bought in airports. I know what you are thinking. "Everything is overpriced in an airport." This is true. But sometimes, you can find just THE right mug that you were waiting for.

So, I have one from the Turkey Starbucks. I have for real stayed and spent time in Turkey so I can count this as a country I have been to, not just an airport I have landed in.

I am so glad I waited and bought this mug from the airport, because, well—I will never forget my airport experience in Turkey.

I was traveling alone, as I usually do. The funny thing is that I had been traveling with a large group of people in Israel, but we had flown back to America separately because I had found the cheapest ticket I could find and was willing to experience the longest layover for the cheapest price. When I had my Turkey airport experience, I cannot really say if I was beyond thrilled that I was no longer traveling with my friends, or sad that they were not there to double over and laugh with me.

"What happened?" you may find yourself asking.

Well, you see—it went like this. I was wearing one of my new favorite LuLaroe maxi skirts. I want to be comfortable when it will take me several days and flights and countries to get home. This skirt was slightly too long for me, but it was cute and comfy, so I was all set.

Or so I thought.

The thing about the Turkey airport is that it is huge. I knew where everything was because I have had several significant layovers there in the past. I knew where the Starbucks was, and I had my eye on the prize to get there.

They have these delightful moving sidewalks there because that airport's "highways and byways" tend to be long. So you can ride/walk/move on those moving sidewalks slightly quicker. There is an unspoken rule that, if you ride, you hang on the right and, if you are walking on the moving sidewalk , you walk to the left of those who are just enjoying the ride.

It took me a bit to understand moving sidewalk etiquette. There should be classes written about things like this.

I figured riding the moving sidewalk was the quickest and most awesome way to get to the Starbucks, because, let's be real, I am still easily amused like a child and find them to be as fun as an amusement park ride.

That is until the amusement park ride goes bad. So, I was doing the walking on the moving sidewalk thing properly in my lane on the left.

Everything was going great until the end of the sidewalk. Remember how I said my oh-so-comfy skirt was just slightly long. The end of my skirt got stuck in the end of the moving sidewalk.

I kept walking with my cute little rolling suitcase (which by the way has four wheels. Can I tell you what a game changer it is having the four wheels on a carry-on? It makes me feel quite deluxe, friends.)

My suitcase and I kept moving, but my skirt did not. It got sucked into the moving sidewalk.

Next thing you know, I am standing in the Turkish airport with people in front of me, behind me, and all around me wondering what in the world to say or do because here I was standing in all my skirtless glory with my awesome four wheeled carry-on suitcase.

I wish you could have seen the faces of those around me. I wish *I* could have seen *my* face.

I could not stop laughing. I figured you laugh or you cry. So, I doubled over laughing. I mean, tears-running-down-the-face laughing. And I think that gave people around me the permission to double over laughing too. After all, if I was laughing, they were not laughing *at* me, they were laughing *with* me.

After I could breathe, I walked back to that moving sidewalk and dug my skirt out. It took quite the finagling, as it had gotten sucked in there good. But a few good tugs and pulls and I was able to put my skirt back on, get back on the moving sidewalk, and get my Starbucks.

And let me tell you, I bought a coffee cup there so that I would not forget that moment. You know what I wanted to remember? That sometimes you just have to laugh, go backwards, pick up the thing that tried to keep you from moving forward, and keep walking.

Because sometimes life will try to suck the life right out of us. The enemy of our souls will try to lie so much to us that the truth just cannot seem to find us.

Have you ever been there? Where you are trying to get somewhere, experience something, make some forward momentum, and everything seems to be keeping you from moving forward?

Maybe it is your own mistakes that have you stuck. Maybe someone else has tripped you up. Either way, we have those moments where all of a sudden we feel super vulnerable. Like parts of us are showing that we do not want to show. Those "what do I do now that I have made a fool of myself in front of all these people?" moments.

John 8 tells us the story of Jesus' encounter with a women who was caught in her sin of adultery. In fact, she was so caught that the Pharisees were all gathered around, ready to stone "such a woman." She was stuck. Stuck in the shame of her sin. And there were people watching, ready to keep her stuck with that label—sinner. Unworthy. Stone her.

Imagine the emotions of that moment. Imagine being that woman. Stuck in shame and pain. Surrounded by people who were watching her, condemning her, telling her she was her past, her mistakes, her pain.

But in steps Jesus. He did what feels like the strangest thing. He just bent down and wrote on the ground. Played in the dirt. But then He said these powerful words.

"But let him who is without sin among you be the first to throw a stone at her."
(John 8:7)

He plays in the dirt some more. And then He said, "Neither do I condemn you; **go,** and sin no more."

Keep moving forward. But this time, move free. Free from sin and shame. Her past was still a part of her, but it was not going to define her. It was her testimony to a God who set her free from sin and shame. She was exposed but free.

Friends, let's do that. The skirtless in Turkey (now, wouldn't that be a fun title for a movie?) moment is still hilarious to me. But it's something I do not want to forget. I could have just stood paralyzed, but I had a destination in mind. So I went back, picked up my skirt, and kept walking.

Keep walking friend. But this time, with your head high remembering that Jesus says, "Go, and sin no more."

That One Time on an Escalator

You may have noticed that I mentioned there was more than one or two times that I have made for some good people-watching material in an airport.

You see, there was that one unfortunate time on the escalator in the Atlanta airport. This incident (I know you will be shocked here, friends) also involved Starbucks.

There seems to be a theme of that in my life.

Starbucks had just come out with their fall drinks—that day. Come on guys. This is a day worth celebrating. So, I had gleefully purchased my grande fall drink and was headed to my gate.

Sure, it probably was not a good idea to think I could balance said drink, maneuver a carry-on suitcase, and try to walk all at the same time. That is just asking too much! And then, throw an escalator into the mix and you cannot even imagine what will happen.

Things started out OK on the top of the escalator as I began my descent. But then I decided to try to take a sip of my Starbucks drink. That's where things got hairy.

The next thing you know, I stumbled. We were halfway down our escalator descent. The coffee went flying out of my hand, and I went forward with my suitcase.

There was, shall we say, a quick domino effect. The coffee first, then me, then my suitcase and all those who were on the steps below me on the escalator. Poor things. They thought they were just in for a normal ride that day. I feel like I know those people now. I am not sure they would call me a friend, but when you find yourself on the ground gazing up at all of those who have also fallen with you, it bonds you somehow.

These new friends were so gracious. Or they just wanted to get away from me. We all kind of checked in with each other. "You OK?" "All your body parts still working?" "Great!"

Then, they went off to their gates and I went off to mine.

However, they did not go off without a memory and a souvenir from me. Each one of them had somehow gotten a bit of my Starbucks drink on them to take with them on the rest of their travels that day.

This is not necessarily the mark I want to leave on people, but I *do* want to leave a mark.

> *"But thanks be to God, who in Christ always leads us in triumphal procession, and through us spreads the fragrance of the knowledge of him **everywhere.** For we are the aroma of Christ to God among those who are being saved and among those who are perishing." (2 Corinthians 2:14)*

I want to be the type of person that, being led by God, spreads the fragrance of Christ everywhere I go.

I don't know about you, but sometimes it can be tempting in my own pride to want to make a name for myself. To be noticed.

That day on the Atlanta airport escalator, I was noticed. I spread some fragrance. (I wonder if there are secret warning signs about me in all the major airports?)

Another time in the Atlanta airport, I was getting Starbucks once again. I was about to sit down and was standing near a railing that overlooked the bottom floor of the airport terminal. I tripped (shocking) and spilled my coffee. I watched in horror as it POURED down over the railing onto the unsuspecting people walking below.

Once again, I left a trail. A fragrance. An imprint.

As much as I love coffee, that's not the imprint I want to make. I want people to know Christ is in a room when I walk in. I want people to want to follow Jesus because I ooze Him wherever I go. I want to shine His light, speak His words, spread His glory story as I got about my story.

What about you, friend? Can we just all stop and think about the "fragrance" we are leaving in a place?

43

Let's stop for a minute and pray. Let's pray that we spread the knowledge of Him everywhere. This world is desperate to know Him. It's desperate to know the hope we have. Would you join me in prayer?

God, You tell us that we are the aroma of Christ. Jesus, would you help me to walk in Your presence, in Your power, and in Your peace in such a way that people around me notice You in me.

Lord, forgive me for wanting to be noticed.

It is truly You, Christ in me, that is the hope of glory. It is no longer I who live, for I have been crucified with Christ. (Galatians 2:20)

Jesus, even when I stumble and fall, will You use me? Will You help make an impact for Your kingdom, everywhere?

P.S. The moral of the story: If you see me in an airport carrying a Starbucks, RUN!

The One Time in First Class

While we are on the topic of airports, can we talk about airplanes? I think I have just as many air*plane* stories as I do air*port* stories. Like the time I accidentally mooned the entire plane because I was wearing a skirt. (Note to self: Jenn, don't wear skirts while traveling.) After much turbulence, I was finally able to leave my seat at the front of the aisle to walk to the bathroom, past ALL the people. My skirt, somehow, had gotten tucked up as I was sitting, and I showed my whole backside to that plane aisle.

44

I only found out the extent of my embarrassment when I was meeting with a publishing agent at the conference I was going to. Apparently, she had been on the plane with me and was like, "Oh, you are the girl that mooned the whole plane."

My very first plane ride was to Japan. Fourteen hours. I mean, why not? Go big or go home.

Luckily, I really enjoyed flying. I learned quickly that an aisle seat was the way to go for my tiny bladder. I have experienced everything from the smoothest of flights to the "I should not have volunteered to sit in the exit row because the turbulence is so bad that I am not at all positive I can actually assist in an emergency like I promised I could so that I could sit in the sit with all the extra leg room" row.

Often in my international travels, I end up going on the long, "you eat way too many airplane meals and watch 17 movies because the flight is so long" type of flights. There was one particular flight where I had been on one plane for 18 long hours, and I knew that as soon as I landed for the next eight hour leg, I only had about a 30 minute layover. I was not really looking forward to that quick turn-around. The idea of cramping my legs back into that tiny space while eating another curry-filled airplane meal was just simply not filling my heart with tons of joy.

I got off the plane, ran to the restroom, and did not even have time to grab coffee before I needed to be on the next flight. (And all the people who have read my coffee-airport-spilling moments say, "AMEN.") When I got to the ticket lady and handed her my ticket to board this flight that I was not excited about getting on, my ticket buzzed, and she said, "Ms. Hand, there has been a ticket change."

I am not going to lie. I inwardly (and maybe outwardly) groaned. I had the feeling that they had changed my seat to the middle of the row of four—the seat of death, in my opinion.

So I walked on the plane, trying to keep my Jesus smile, but definitely not feeling it. I started to walk back into Coach, because well , that's where I go on a plane. The flight attendant stopped me and said, "Right this way, Ms. Hand."

WHAT!?!?! She directed me through the magic curtain to the other side. I promise there were angels singing the most beautiful version of the "Hallelujah Chorus" as the curtain parted and she escorted me to FIRST CLASS. (Yes, that needs to be in all caps here, friends!) I had no idea why or how, all I knew is that, all of a sudden, my seat had gotten quite the upgrade. When I looked at the First Class seat, I realized it made into a bed.

As I sat in my luxurious seat-bed, several shocking things happened. First, they handed me a robe and slippers. For real. Like we were at a spa, not about to be suspended in the air for the next eight hours in a tin can. It was the most luxurious robe and slippers I have ever put on. Then the flight attendant asked me if I would like a mint julep. I didn't even know what that meant, but I was like, "Bring it on." She then handed me a menu card with five courses and asked me to circle which thing I would like at each course. I had no idea what most of these things were. All I could remember were the boxy tray curry meals I had in my last eighteen hours in coach.

I giggled like a school girl the whole time. This was the upgrade of a lifetime. On these overseas flights, these first class tickets cost thousands of dollars more. I had no idea what I was doing there in First Class. I kept thinking, "I am going to be found out." And then I was thinking, "I sure do wish I had a friend here to enjoy this with me."

I smiled the entire eight hours. I put my chair in every position it could go. I loved that I had my own personal stewardess. For real, her only job was to cater to my every need. I am not a needy person, and well, I had never done anything like this, so I was probably a pretty easy one for her. Especially since I literally giggled the whole time.

They brought the best food I have ever had in my life for me to eat. Six courses of it with palate cleansers in between (whatever that means). No barely-room-for-a-small-cup-of-orange-juice tray table for me. In first class, there was this awesome little table that they pulled out, and no kidding, my personal stewardess placed a white tablecloth on it and set it with fine china for my little six course meal.

Whose life was I living?

At one point, because you are much closer to the pilot up there in First Class, the pilot came out to greet us and thank us for flying with them. I kept thinking, "At what point are they going to figure out I do not belong here? I do not deserve to be here. I am a coach girl not a fancy flier."

It was the most glorious eight hours. I could not figure out how to keep the real coffee cup they give you to drink coffee in. (I figured it would be awkward and weird if I asked.) But I did keep the coffee stirring spoon.

Sometimes I get it out and stir my coffee with it to remind me of the time I got to go "behind the curtain" and enjoy things First Class.

Behind the Veil

Things were very different there, behind the First Class curtain. You were closer to the pilot. You had your own personal stewardess. You had room to breathe. They called you by name.

In the temple in the Old Testament days, there was an area called this Holy of Holies. This was an area that contained the Ark of the Covenant. This sacred place represented the presence of God. It was separated from the rest of the temple by a curtain that only the High Priest could enter, once a year, on the Day of Atonement. On this day, the High Priest would enter this holy place and make atonement for the sins of the people.

Behind this curtain represented the presence of God. The forgiveness of God. The holiness of God. And you and I could not go there.

Matthew 27:51 tells us that after Jesus died, the veil (or curtain) of the Holy of Holies was torn in two from top to bottom. That which was separating the people from the Presence was torn.

GLORY!!! (That is glory-shouting stuff, friends).

*"Therefore, brothers, since we have confidence to enter the holy places by the blood of Jesus, by the new and living way that he opened for us **through the curtain,** that is, through his own flesh, and since we have a great high priest over the house of God, let us draw near with a true heart in full assurance of faith, with our hearts sprinkled clean from an evil conscience and our bodies washed with pure water. Let us hold fast the confession of our hope without wavering, for He who promised is faithful." (Hebrews 10:19-23)*

We were invited into First Class. When Jesus died and resurrected three days later, our ticket was changed. No more coach for us. No more having to have a priest go into the presence of God for us.

The curtain was torn. Our invitation was signed in the blood of Jesus. Invited. In.

With this ticket change, we have closer access to the Pilot. We have been called by name. Isaiah 43 tells us that He has called us by name; we are His.

He who promised is faithful. We did not deserve it. We did not pay the First Class price. He did. For you.

So, why cram yourself in the coach seats, thinking the presence of God is far too unattainable for you? Why settle for small, tiny-tray, box meals when you can dine with the King of Kings?

He has invited you in.

"How much more will the blood of Christ, who through the eternal Spirit offered himself without blemish to God, purify our conscience from dead works to serve the living God."
(Hebrews 9:14)

Slip on your robe of righteousness. Lean back into all the space at the throne of grace. Grab your coffee spoon and taste and see that the Lord is good. (And you may as well giggle a little.)

Chapter Six

On Travel Mugs

Just so you know, the travel mugs are not counted in my mug collection because they are a whole separate category. They get their own cabinet.

Can you please tell me you have this problem also? It seems the to-go mugs always manage to go into the car and never seem to end up back in the house where they started. Please tell me I am not alone in this. It will come clean-out-the-car time and it looks like I run my own traveling coffee shop.

That, plus the fact that I have spilled coffee so often in my car that it has that "old gas station coffee" smell to it. Just this week in fact, I hit the horn while trying to open my coffee lid and use the steering wheel at the same time. It startled me, so I screamed and my coffee went everywhere. So much for those yummy first sips. They were now all over the car.

I have a variety of travel mugs. The "not necessarily the cutest but guaranteed to keep your coffee hot for your ten hour trip" coffee mugs. Then there are the cute, "I am not going far and when I walk in a place I want to have my cute coffee mug" ones.

Then there is my favorite one - a homemade wood one. It is beautiful. Every year for Christmas, our family makes one homemade gift and buys a thrift store gift and a ten dollar gift for whichever name that you draw. It's so fun because it keeps the gifts simple and meaningful.

My dad was determined to make me a coffee mug one year. He has a wooden lathe turner thing (I am for sure that is the official technical name), and he started working on the coffee mug. We joked because he gave me an IOU certificate that first year, saying he was still working on it. *Three years later*, I got the most beautiful wood travel mug. I treasure it because it was made by my incredible dad's own hands. Whenever I take it out places, people ask if they can put an order in to buy one. I always laugh and say, "Sure. Be ready to receive it in nine years."

I wanted to include this chapter because I wanted to talk about God's provision. I imagine there is someone that is reading this that, at some point, had a need and wondered how God is going to provide. When we become overwhelmed by our need, it can be easy to quickly become underwhelmed by the power of God to provide. I am not saying health, wealth, and prosperity gospel here. But I can testify, and I know you can too, of a God who provides.

You see, my travel mugs need a *car* to travel in. It's kind of a thing. Each time I slip a coffee mug into my cup holder for a trip, whether it's a trip to Aldi with my quarter ready to buggy rent or it's a four hundred mile drive to go to a speaking engagement, my car is a sweet reminder of the provision of God.

Opal the Odyssey

I had this car named Toby the Taurus. I do not know if you are a car namer, but I am. I grew up in a family that named most of our inanimate objects, including things like our big Shop Vac. Before I can tell you about Opal the Odyssey, let me tell you about Toby the Taurus. Toby was the car I drove after getting back from living overseas in Nepal. I loved Toby.

Really, I did. But Toby the Taurus kept my prayer life in serious business. Like, I pretty much had to hit my knees every time I wanted to go anywhere and pray I would get there.

There was a time that whenever I wanted to go anywhere, I had to unplug the battery when I got to a place and plug it back in when it was time to go. How professional does that look when you are coming to speak?

I started to realize Toby was on his last leg. All the "check engine" lights were on all the time. This made it tricky to get my car tags renewed, because I could not pass the emissions test. This also resulted in my expired tags getting me a very expensive ticket at Sonic Happy Hour where I was getting my diet coke with extra lime.

The police officer that was parked in the stall next to mine turned his blue lights on, walked over to my car, and "pulled me over," writing me a super-expensive ticket. I wish he had just enjoyed his hot dog without looking over.

One particular weekend I was driving to a retreat I was working when Toby the Taurus decided he didn't want to go over forty miles an hour anymore. That is not ideal on the interstate. So, we trudged and limped to the camp. I am not going to lie. I live on a missionary budget. I am single, so I do not have a rich husband to fall back on. I live by faith in a God who provides, but that weekend I was weary. I was thinking, "What are you going to do this time, Lord?"

Honestly, it was not in a faith-filled, "I cannot wait to see you provide and move in this situation" kind of way. It was an "I am trying not to worry but I **need a car that goes over 40 mph Lord"** desperate kind of prayer.

The theme that weekend was "nothing is impossible with God." Over and over that weekend, I heard this verse:

*"Blessed is she who **believed** there would be a fulfillment of that which was spoken to her from the Lord." (John 1:45)*

I was puttering home with Toby the Taurus after the incredible retreat, praying I would make it home, when I got a phone call from a dear friend. She said the dreaded words, "I need to talk to you." My mind of course automatically went to something was wrong. Although I was exhausted and honestly not really up for company, I told her to come over to my house right away.

I made it home, and she came over. We did the chit-chat thing, and I kept wondering when she was going to tell me the real reason she had wanted to come over. All of a sudden, there was a knock on the door. I inwardly groaned because I was exhausted and not sure I wanted more people over. I opened the door and a couple who are dear friends of mine were standing there. We all made small talk and then, out of nowhere, they teared up. They said, "Jenn, we have something for you."

I have not been speechless many times in my life, but I was in that moment. Because they handed me the keys and a title to their Honda Odyssey minivan.

I am tearing up just thinking about it. The exact time that Toby the Taurus was breaking down, God told them to give me this van.

When Mary was told by an angel she was going to carry Jesus, the son of God, she said, "Nothing is impossible with God."

Nothing is impossible with God. Do you need that reminder today? I just felt like someone that is reading this might. You might need to hear a story of God's faithfulness to remind you that He is working behind the scenes. He sees the need that is keeping you up at night. He showed me that night the impossible made possible.

We named her Opal the Odyssey. I loved her so much. Every time I put the key in the ignition, I sensed the Lord whisper, "I see you, Jenn. I know you, Jenn. I love you, Jenn."

Since there are so many Honda Odysseys in the world, I put a bright purple spikey steering wheel cover on her that I got for 99 cents at Goodwill. I drove Opal all over the country and loved her and her purple-steering-wheel-covered self.

Catrina the Camry

You would think that I would have learned my faith lesson there with the miraculous exact moment I needed provision of Opal the Odyssey. But well, isn't it funny how we can quickly forget that God is a God of miracles, not just of one time, but all the time?

They come in all different shapes and sizes. All different answers to prayer. Not always the way we think they will come. But He is a God of miracles.

So as I am typing this, I am listening to a random playlist on Spotify and the song playing right now is declaring, "I believe in You. I believe in You. You're the God of miracles."

Amen.

Opal the Odyssey was awesome for so many years. However, this year, I was driving up a mountain to our beginning-of-the-year Coming Alive Ministries board meeting. She began to slip and make this crazy "the engine is about to fall out" sound. I knew in my gut this was not good. That it probably was the transmission making not-so-good transmission sounds.

I made it to the board meeting. However, on the way home, Opal gave up on the way down the mountain. Even in that moment, God provided. My sister was right behind me and was able to pick me up. My van broke down right in front a friend's laundry mat, so I was able to leave Opal there for the night. And although it did not break down in my town, it broke down in a town that I had spent a great deal of time in, and where my dad just so happened to know a mechanic that he trusted.

So the next morning, poor Opal got towed to the car hospital to find out just what was wrong. My sweet friend picked me up that day to run some errands and hang out. She also knew I was a bit stressed about this whole car situation, because I had a feeling in my gut it was going to be something too expensive for me to get fixed.

There is something about car problems that makes a girl feel extra single. I mean, I know where to put most all of the fluids thanks to Toby the Taurus. But I don't know the car mechanic lingo. It's hard to know what decisions to make. I told my friend Casey, "I can do without most anything, but I hope God knows I need a car to do what He has called me to do."

Do you hear the whiney, panicky tone in my voice there—because it was there? It is amazing how quickly I forgot the amazing provision of God.

I will never forget the moments that happened next. We had run into CVS drugstore to pick up something for Casey. She was talking to the pharmacist and my phone rang. It was the mechanic.

I quickly grabbed a sheet of pharmacy notepaper and wrote down the numbers he was giving me. It's never good when the mechanic tells you that you might want to sit down.

"Ms. Hand, it's the transmission. Here are the numbers. The absolute cheapest we can do is $3,959.00."

I wrote this number down and then I am going to admit. My "normally calm about everything, nothing really phases me" manner diminished quickly. I dissolved into tears (which is unusual for me). Like "sobbing in the medicine aisle" tears. I grabbed the keys and ran to Casey's car.

I had a conversation with God where I reminded him, "Don't You know that I do ministry FOR YOU? Don't You know that I am single with limited resources? Don't You know I need a car and I for sure don't have the money to fix this one?"

I think it may have been a moment similar to one Hagar had. Hagar was Sarah's maidservant. When Abraham saw that Sarah was not having success bearing him children, they decided that Hagar was the answer. (Sometimes the Bible seems like an episode in a reality television show.) Hagar did have a son, and then, as you can imagine, Sarah (called Sarai at the time, just for details' sake) got jealous. She went a little "mean girl" on Hagar.

So Hagar ran. And she found herself in the wilderness. I cannot imagine the emotions she was going through. Maybe similar to what I felt when I was in the CVS that day. "Don't you see me Lord?"

An angel of the Lord came to visit Hagar there in the wilderness by the spring. He reminded her that God saw her, that God was with her, that He was looking after her.

*"So she called the name of the Lord who spoke to her, 'You are a **God of seeing**,' for she said, 'Truly here I have seen him who looks after me.'" (Genesis 16:13)*

I am so grateful that we have a God of seeing. I have the piece of paper from CVS taped above my desk to always remind me of that. He saw me crying in the CVS that day. He sees you right in the middle of your mundane day. He sees you in your moments of fear. He sees you as you rejoice. He sees you in the moments of despair. He is there.

Can I tell you how amazing God is? My sweet friends invited me to come to their house that night to borrow their car for as long as I needed. These particular friends have been such mentors to my life and have been a huge part of Coming Alive Ministries. Remember my friend who came to my house the night that I was given Opal the Odyssey?

She offered to drive me to my friends' house to get the car they were going to let me borrow. We went in our friends' house and, after chatting for a little while, my friend got tears in his eyes. He said, "Jenn, we have talked it over. We want to not just let you borrow this car. We want to give it to you!"

Am I on a game show here, friends? Car number two? This deserves bold ALL CAPS GLORY SHOUTING!

We all cried. I could not believe how quickly God had answered my desperate prayer.

I now am the proud owner of a white Camry with a sunroof. I love her. I named her Catrina the Camry in honor of my friend Catrina who had been with me both times I had been offered a car.

I don't know your need right now. But this I know. The enemy tries to tempt us all into those Hagar moments. Those "in the wilderness wondering where God is" moments. Those moments when it's hard to whisper even desperate prayers.

My friends, the truth is there is a God who sees.

Chapter Seven

Manifesto Life

My name is Jenn and I am a cheesy holiday celebrator. Anyone else here? I love all things holiday. I love tradition and family and hospitality. I love the smells that come with the seasons. It all starts with fall in my opinion and goes uphill from there. I realize fall is a season not a holiday, but it feels like it ushers in the holidays to me, so I am just going to call it that.

I am one of those pumpkin-spice-everything lovers. Especially the candles. I love the candles. Which understandably makes my friends and my landlord nervous because I have been known to light things on fire accidentally more times than I can count.

I may or may not have a few fall coffee mugs. Truthfully, they do not have a great story or memory in them like the rest. They only survived the Great Coffee Cup Purge because I count fall as one big giant memory. And I have a rule. No drinking from these mugs until fall. Who knew that coffee mugs have rules? I will let you in on another one of my coffee mug rules. I cannot drink from the same one in a week. New day=new cup. Or, if I drink more than one cup a day (which, may I confess, happens often and I am sure you are shocked), I cannot use the same mug from earlier that day. Each mug needs a chance to feel loved. Mug love.

I am so grateful we have a God who makes seasons that change. I think it is a sweet representation of the seasons in our lives. I am also so thankful that, although seasons change, our God does not.

"Every good and every perfect gift is from above, coming down from the Father of lights with whom there is no variation or shadow due to change." (James 1:17)

One morning, I was trying to make my own version of a pumpkin spice latte using actual pumpkin spice in the little shaker can. Keep in mind, this was pre-coffee. I liberally sprinkled…A LOT.

Imagine my surprise when it was not pumpkin spice at all. It was curry powder. I had liberally sprinkled curry powder in my coffee. Let's just say it did not have quite the "fall party in your mouth" feeling I was going for.

While we are talking about that, can I tell you about the time I had not put my contacts in yet, and had just taken my glasses off to wash my face and decided to brush my teeth? I grabbed what I thought was toothpaste, but in reality, it was Benadryl cream. A nice squirt of that on my toothbrush was its own party in my mouth.

Back to seasons. I want to be a celebrator of life. I want to live alive. (That's why I named my ministry Coming Alive.) I do not want to miss the majestic because I get sucked into a life of mundane.

I want to turn my mundane moments into worshiping-His-majesty moments. I want to celebrate. The Bible is full of celebrations. In fact, they had mandatory celebrations, feasts, times set aside to dance, to play, to fellowship, and worship the One who had freed them.

There was a particular season of my life when I felt like I was numb and bored. Nothing necessarily was wrong, I just had gotten caught in the business of busy. I was doing what needed to be done. I am sure you know that feeling. The "days are just going by so fast that I am not sure where they went, but I am not sure where my soul went either" type of season.

I decided I wanted to do something about that. It was nearing fall so I decided to write what I called my Fall Manifesto.

The definition of manifesto is "a written statement that describes the policies, goals, and opinions of a person or a group."

This sounds a little dry and boring for me, frankly. But I wanted to write something for that season that would help me *enjoy* the moments instead of *missing* the moments.

So I got some fun paper and a pretty pen, of course, and wrote out my Fall Manifesto. I will not call it a goal list, because that takes all of the fun out of it. But it was a list of things I wanted to enjoy, savor, and participate in that season. These things covered all the things. Some were spiritual goals, some were physical goals, and most were fun "enjoyment of all things fall" goals.

Bonfires, s'mores, pumpkin patches with the nieces and nephew, learning to make pumpkin chili—these were some of the items on my manifesto.

Then there was go on a personal spiritual retreat, memorize a new Bible verse a week, and fill out a gratitude journal.

These all made the manifesto.

I thought it was fun so I had my Bible study ladies do this Fall Manifesto writing exercise. It was so fun to share with each other how we were going to intentionally come alive by living moments fully alive. Taking time to savor. And as we savored moments, experiencing the Savior in those moments.

This practice stuck. Now at the turn of every season, we write a manifesto for that season. I think it would be so fun if you would try this with me. If you do, I would love for you to document it on social media (because, I mean, did it really happen if it is not on social media?) with the hashtag #seasonsofmanifesto.

Chapter Eight

Donkeys and Camels

The last time I was in Israel, I had the most hilarious moment with a camel, and I am now the proud owner of a mug with a camel on it. My friends wanted me to pay to ride the camel. But I just decided I was not going to do it. The last time I had paid to ride an animal things went a little crazy. I will tell you more about that later. I like to keep you on the edge of your seat.

I did tell my friends if they would take a picture, I would kiss the camel.

I don't think they believed me, but I was not fooling around, folks. I am willing to do anything for a great picture. I mean, who doesn't want a camel-kissing-picture from Jerusalem? That's almost as good as an airbrushed t-shirt.

So I leaned in for a kiss with the camel. I stayed there and lingered, only because I could not hear my friend David Disney say he had taken the picture. I am not sure I have ever heard him laugh so hard when he said, "Jenn, enough already. I took the picture." The camel and I were both glad when this moment was over.

The camel kissing moment reminded me of my donkey riding experience. I am always up for an adventure. This particular day (this was in an entirely different country from the camel kissing country, by the way) it seemed like such a fun day to have a donkey-riding adventure. A friend and I were in a third world country walking around by the ocean. There were a few men there that had donkeys that were available to ride for a small fee.

I mean, what doesn't seem cooler than riding on a donkey in the sand right where the ocean's tide gently comes rushing in? It was not a "knight in shining armor on a white horse" kind of moment, more like a donkey in the dirt—but it sounded like fun.

So my friend and I paid to ride the donkeys. I was a little nervous when I looked at my donkey. My donkey looked slightly malnourished. And, well, I am not.

But the idea of the adventure overtook any practical thinking, so I was in. Donkey paid for. Saddled up (or whatever in the world you say when you get ready to ride a donkey).

Things were going great. It was so fun. Clip clop clip clop slowly through the sand, the ocean waves lapping at the donkey's feet. Sure ,my donkey was a little slow, but that's OK. Well, it was OK at first.

That is until all of a sudden, my donkey stopped. Friends, it didn't just stop moving. Before I knew how to say, "glory" I was in the water. Those waves were now lapping over me, the sand sticking to me.

My donkey had fallen over. Not just fallen over to get back up. My malnourished donkey had *died*.

Right there with me on its back.

My donkey had died. I am still not sure to laugh or cry at this but laughter always prevails.

The donkey's owner was none too happy that somehow I had killed his donkey, so he did not go for giving me the "I didn't get my full ride" refund.

Now you understand why I turned down the camel ride in Jerusalem?

Carrying the Messiah

The Bible does not specifically tell us, but I am almost positive when Mary was very pregnant and making the journey from Nazareth to Bethlehem she would have ridden on a donkey. For her sake, since she was pregnant, I hope her donkey was not malnourished, taking her on this journey. (P.S. Can you imagine donkey riding while very pregnant?) The donkey was carrying the one who was carrying the Messiah.

Mark 11 tells us of another time the Messiah was carried by a donkey.

"Now when they drew near to Jerusalem, to Bethpage and Bethany, at the Mount of Olives, Jesus sent two of his disciples and said to them, 'Go into the village in front of you, and immediately as you enter it you will find a donkey tied, on which no one has ever sat. Untie it, and bring it. If anyone says to you, 'Why are you doing this?' say, 'The Lord has need of it and will send it back her immediately.'" And they went away and found a colt tied at a door outside in the street, and they untied it. And some of those standing there said to them, 'What are you doing, untying the colt?' And they told them what Jesus had said, and they let them go. And they brought the colt to Jesus and threw their cloaks on it, and he sat on it. And many spread their cloaks on the road, and others spread leafy branches that they had cut from the fields. And those who went before and those who followed were shouting, 'Hosanna! Blessed is he who comes in the name of the Lord! Blessed is the coming kingdom of our Father David! Hosanna in the highest!'"

Palm branches and spreading your cloak. That was a reception reserved for a king. A Messiah.

Once again, a donkey was carrying the message of the Messiah. They were not shouting, "Hosanna" to worship the donkey—they were proclaiming that a king was coming.

Friends, we get to be like the donkey. Now I know calling ourselves a donkey doesn't seem very flattering. Stick with me here.

A donkey carried Mary who was carrying the Messiah.

A donkey carried the Messiah on the Palm Sunday walk.

We get to carry the Messiah in our everyday walk.

A carrier of the Good News. A carrier of the Gospel. A carrier of the King.

What a glorious calling.

"But we have this treasure in jars of clay, to show that the surpassing power belongs to God and not to us...always carrying in us the death of Jesus, so that the life of Jesus may also be manifested in our bodies." (2 Corinthians 4:7,10)

Chapter Nine

Endings and Confessions

Honestly, I find the idea of writing the end of a book the most intimidating. OK, let me be completely truthful. I find writing *any* part of a book intimidating. Give me a microphone and I come alive. Ask me to sit and be quiet and write—well, the extrovert in me wonders if I will shrivel up and die.

And then there is the fear-of-rejection part of me. The "what will people think?" part of me. The "what if they don't like me, and they write a bad review on Amazon?" part of me.

I mean, those five little stars on Amazon reviews - where you can pick one, two, three, four, or five stars - could literally paralyze me.

Because, frankly, I am a people-pleaser. Or shall I say, a recovering people-pleaser? I feel like my thirties have been my favorite years of my life. Because with each passing year (why do I feel like a grandma writing that?), I feel like God plants deeper and deeper in my heart the truth of how much He loves me. How much it's not about me at all—it's about the Christ *in* me.

Every year I pick a word for the year. January 1st is one of my favorite days of the year. I am the cheesiest, love all things Christmas girl there is, so it's always nice in the days after Christmas to at least look forward to the next year. To a brand new calendar of pages to dream and to prepare for what God may have in store.

When it comes to word picking time, I just pray. And try to listen. That is unless God gives me a word like "suffering." Then I am like, "Um, I don't think I heard You right on that one, Lord." (Just kidding. I do try to be open-minded to whatever word the Lord wants to give me. Well, mostly.)

This year, I felt strongly the word the Lord gave me was "believe." And then He added another word, "risk." That to *believe* was going to require *risk*. I do not know about you, but I find that when I believe, I have to hope, and hope can sometimes feel risky. It feels risky because we do not know the outcome.

Sometimes, believing God looks like taking big, risky steps of obedience to the call of God.

Take Abraham for example. Belief meant going to a nation he did not know. He only knew that he was called to go.

Belief meant trusting in a promise for a son when he was old enough for the nursing home. Risking what others thought. Risking hope.

"No distrust made him waver concerning the promises of God, but he grew strong in his faith as he gave glory to God, fully convinced that God was able to do what he had promised." (Romans 4:20)

What strong words. Oh Lord, please make this me. Where no distrust makes me waver concerning the promises of God, but I will grow strong in my faith, giving glory to God, fully convinced that I can trust Him.

(Taking a dramatic pause there to let that prayer of my heart sink in for me. Maybe you need that, too. And just so you know, I was sipping my sleepy time tea because well, it's sleepy time. As I wrote that prayer, I got so excited that I fell off the high-top stool I am sitting on, dropping me and my tea, hence the need for the dramatic pause. Just wanted to clearly set the scene for you.)

This year as I was doing the pray for a word thing, I was filling out this awesome goal setting planner. I know, friends. Those of you that know me are shocked and confused right now. *Jenn, a planner filler-outer. I cannot even imagine it.*

Truthfully, it still shocks me. But this one is different. It has stickers and no real calendar. And it's pretty.

One of the things at the first of the year that it had you fill out was a page on what are you afraid of. There were spaces to list four fears.

I thought in all my prideful self, "I am a pretty fearless girl. Whatever will I fill these lines with?"

So I prayed and wrote the first thing that came to my mind.

Fear of failure.

Oh. OK. There's that. And then I wrote the second thing that came to my mind. Fear of success.

Hmm…it would seem that these two fears coupled together would leave me with one result - stuck in between.

This was a huge revelation of what was going on in my heart. And why I believe God gave me the word "believe" coupled with the word "risk."

Because it was going to take exercising some faith muscles. Some belief in my heart and my mind which would lead to taking risk in my actions of obedient faith. It would mean some failure. It would mean maybe some success. But, heaven knows, I sure don't want to stay stuck and stalled because of the "in-between."

What about you?

So let me pause here and check in with you. I feel like I just did a lot of talking right there. And well, I literally did talk out loud as I wrote, because I have been home with the stomach bug the past few days and have not seen other humans, and I needed to use my extrovert voice.

It's your turn. It may or may not be the new year as you read these words. But let's pretend it is. Let's pretend you have a blank sheet of paper and you are praying for a word or a phrase from the Lord for your year.

And maybe you already did that. If so, here is some time to pause and check-in. How has God worked that word into your heart and your life this year?

If you have not done it, what better time than now? Make sure you have some good inspirational music playing in the background, of course. And in the ideal world, you will have a lovely pen that you enjoy writing with. One of my first retail jobs in graduate school was at a school supply store where I fell in love with pens. (Side note: That store, oh my goodness, still used Apple computers and not the Mac kind. I promise it was not in the 80s - I was only a wee baby then. It was way past time to be using those kind.)

So, get your favorite pen and paper, and ask the Lord for your word. (Gosh, I felt really bossy there. I mean, just because it's the end of the book, I promise I am not getting all bossy on you now. I just, well—got excited.) So I am saying it in my most non-bossy, "I have a counseling degree...how does that make you feel?" tone.

Ask the Lord for a word. And can I give you permission to know that you may not hear it at once? You may feel like all you hear is silence. That's OK. We're all friends here. Just keep asking. Praying. Seeking.

Go on a walk in nature.

Go have coffee with a friend.

Do something that makes you come alive. And as you do, listen for what you sense God is speaking to your heart.

While you are seeking, why don't you do that same little "four places for your fears" exercise I was telling you about? (You may be like, "Jenn, I need way more than four lines." That's OK. Feel free to use as many as you like.)

What are you afraid of? Would you be willing to take that word God gave you, along with the fears you are recognizing, to the Word? Search through the living, active word of God for passages that speak of that word and that fear. I believe God wants to do some crazy, awesome things in your heart.

For example, I was looking up my word for the year just this week and found the story of a man who brought his son to Jesus. He told Jesus, "I believe; help my unbelief."

I love that. I want that. I pray that. I believe; help my unbelief. And, because I believe, show me how to have risky faith. Faith that obeys. Water-walking faith. That when Jesus says, "Come," I do. When Jesus says, "Go!" I go. When Jesus says, "Stay and love your neighbor," I stay and love my neighbor.

When Jesus says to write a book and don't stay stuck in the in-between, I get to typing.

You see, I have this crazy dream of having a traditionally published book. If you are not into the publishing world (which probably the majority of you do not feel the need to be), traditional publishers pay you to write a book. Then your book gets in all the bookstores in real life. You have a marketing team and editor and fancy cover creators. The author still works just as hard; it just is done on more of the traditional writing route.

In the publishing world, you have to have numbers to get numbered. The buzz word is "platform."

You have to build a platform, a tribe. And I get it. They are using the big bucks on you. It makes sense to me.

My books have all been self-published. That means you pay individual people to do those things. Edit the text, design the cover, format the pages, and all the other things.

So, I have a dream of working in the traditional publishing world. I feel the Lord has deposited that seed of faith in me. That someday that will happen for a book He has called me to write. And this year, with the word *risk*, the Lord has asked me to take some steps of faith and obedience in that direction. In some ways, these steps seemed big and scary. Because what if I fail? (My first thought.) And what if I succeed? (My second thought.)

Here is the conclusion I had to come to - what if I simply obey God, believe, risk and, like Abraham, trust the outcome?

Take the steps. And wait for the results. And until then, self-publish these words, because this book and these words were burning within me, especially as I thought of celebrating five years of Coming Alive Ministries.

Five years of God taking this crazy, unorganized girl and letting her be the Executive Director (which really just means I get a fun coffee cup with our logo on it) of this ministry. Most of the time, I have NO idea what I am doing, but Jesus takes me step by step. And when I stumble and fall or stall— He is with me through it all.

OK, guys—that was quite the rhymer, wasn't it?

And let me tell you, I have fallen—like, for real, *fallen* a few times. It seems to happen every time I try to be all cool and swanky and speak in high heels. I usually can make it as a high-heel-wearing poser for a few sessions when I am speaking, but there is always that point when I get excited about what I am saying and fall right over.

How does one professionally recover from that?

Or, how does one recover from the time you are speaking at the conference where you used your really cool vintage bicycle as the décor? You were bringing the conference to an end. You know the point where the Spirit has moved, the Lord has spoken, people are teary eyed, and you are inviting them to Jesus.

And then you somehow push over the bike, which pushes over the other decorations and everything goes crashing, including you—and you cannot pull yourself together again from laughing.

I may or may not have experienced that.

I am learning to keep risking. Keep believing. Keep typing. Keep praying. Keep walking/sometimes running/sometimes baby-stepping to that which I feel God calling is calling me.

Can I cheer you on in that? Can I encourage you in that? See, it seems appropriate that, as I was typing the last words of the last chapter of this book, I got a package in the mail from my dear friend, Catrina. In that package was the most beautiful coffee mug.

Yes, that makes coffee mug number 58. (OK, truthfully, I have gotten a few mugs since I began working on this book, so it may actually be number 62.) It's huge. It's the perfect coffee-snuggling mug.

It's white and it says on it, "Philippians 4:13." And I needed that right at these moments. These "I am about to finish this book, push send, and will publish it to the world" moments. In case you need a refresher, here is what Philippians 4:13 says:

"I can do all things through Christ who strengthens me."

Friends, can we just shout that together? Can we let that settle deep down in our hearts? This truth is so freeing, because the strength is not about me. It's about Christ who strengthens me.

Christ who strengthens you. The verses surrounding this don't often make the coffee cup.

"Not that I am speaking of being in need, for I have learned in whatever situation I am to be content. I know how to be brought low, and I know how to abound. In any and every circumstance, I have learned the secret of facing plenty and hunger, abundance and need." (Philippians 4:11-12)

Do you happen to notice something there? Paul is saying he has learned how to succeed and to fail. He has learned to have much and how to have little.

He has learned to be content.

Why? Because of Christ who strengthens him.

Nothing brings strength to my day like a good, strong cup of dark coffee. But nothing brings strength to my heart like a dose of Jesus.

A dose of the one who took nails and a crown of thorns and a spear through His side so that that I can be free.

The secret of coming alive and living fully alive? Christ.

The inside of this coffee cup that my friend gave me says, "Enjoy life." These are the words that come straight to your eyes when you tip the cup forward to drink of the coffee goodness.

Remember the cup of suffering we talked about in the Garden of Gethsemane. Jesus drank that so we could enjoy life.

Remember the cup He passed His disciples saying, "This is my blood spilled for you...This is my body broken for you...Do this in remembrance of me."

Would you take a moment to take the cup, tip it up, let these words come straight to your heart as you tip it up to drink of the goodness of the Lord?

Enjoy life.

Come alive.

Live fully alive.

Because Christ is alive. And He offers you life. John 10:10 says "I have come that you may have life and life abundantly."

Do you find yourself afraid today? Take those fears to Him, and let Him speak lovingly to them.

Are you wondering what the next steps are? Take those steps to Him and let Him guide you through them.

Are you stuck, stalled, feeling silenced by your situation? Let His love seek you out.

Let Him fight for you. Let Him love you. Let Him give you peace. Let Him convict you. Let Him free you. Let Him cover you. Let Him forgive you. Let Him secure you. Let Him strengthen you.

The God who designed your moments is collecting them with you.

Grab a mug and let's celebrate.

Made in the USA
Columbia, SC
14 October 2017